A JEW ON ETHIOPIA STREET

Allan Havis

BROADWAY PLAY PUBLISIIING INC
New York
www.broadwayplaypublishing.com
info@broadwayplaypublishing.com

A JEW ON ETHIOPIA STREET
© Copyright 2012 by Allan Havis

First printing: June 2012
I S B N: 978-0-88145-533-5

Book design: Marie Donovan
Page make-up: Adobe Indesign
Typeface: Palatino
Printed and bound in the U S A

ABOUT THE AUTHOR

Productions by Allan Havis at San Diego Rep, Old Globe, Vox Nova, Seattle's A C T, Long Wharf, South Coast Rep, American Repertory Theater, Hartford Stage, Virginia Stage, Berkshire Theater Festival, Philadelphia Theater Co, and Rowholt Theater-Verlag (National German Radio). Commissions include England's Chichester Festival, Sundance, San Diego Rep, Ted Danson's Anasazi Productions, South Coast Rep, Mixed Blood, C S C Rep, Malashock Dance, & Carolina Chamber Chorale. With over 16 plays in print, other publications include a novel *Albert the Astronomer, American Political Plays* (2001), *American Political Plays After 9/11* (2010), & *Cult Films: Taboo & Transgression*, (2008). In collaboration with composer Anthony Davis, their opera *Lilith* premiered at U C San Diego's Conrad Prebys Hall in 2009 and their second opera *Lear On The 2nd Floor* premiered at Princeton's McCarter Theater in 2012. Recipient of Guggenheim, Rockefeller, Kennedy Center/American Express, C B S, H B O, National Endowment for the Arts Awards, & San Diego Theater Critics Circle. He earned an M F A from Yale. He is provost of Thurgood Marshall College/U C San Diego and a professor of Theater.

A JEW ON ETHIOPIA STREET was commissioned by Mixed Blood Theater (Jack Reuler, Artistic Director) in Minneapolis. The play was subsequently produced at Mixed Blood Theater in March 2001 with the following cast and creative contributors:

EZRA SHLOMO.. Marvin Grays
SONYA GELMAN... Meri Golden
ETI SHLOMO .... Togba Norris
HESHI LEOWITZ..Clyde Lund
FISHMAN...Joe Minjares
RONIT MELKAV..Jodi Kellogg
DELAL SHLOMO .... Regina Marie Williams
SHEVA ADDA ....Antu Yacob

Director..Michael Kissin
Sets.. Jeff Thomson
Lights .... Paul Epton
Sound ....Andrew Meyer
Costumes.. Barb Portinga
Stage manager..Robin Macgregor

CHARACTERS & SETTING

EZRA SHLOMO, *Ethiopian born, 40s, Israeli Absorption Center Official*

SONYA GELMAN, *Russian born, 40s, Israeli Absorption Center Official*

ETI SHLOMO, *Ethiopian born, 18, athlete, in Israel 4 years.*

HESHI LEBOWITZ, *Ashkanazie Jew, 60s, diamond cutter and merchant*

FISHMAN, *American sports czar, 50s, with Israeli residency*

RONIT MELKAV, *Israeli university official, 40s, friendly with* FISHMAN.

DELAL SHLOMO, ETI's *mother, Ethiopian, 40s, not assimilated to Israel.*

SHEVA ADDA, ETI's *girlfriend, Ethiopian, 17, still in high school*

The play is set in Jerusalem, from January to March 1996.

There are 20 scenes. Folk and contemporary Ethiopian music is heard between scenes, featuring some music sung by SHEVA *in designated scenes and as segue-ways.*

to Anne Porter for so much help and wisdom at
Marshall College and for splendid friendship

Scene One

(SHEVA, *in a simple red dress and microphone in hand,
finishes a romantic song. There is warm applause. Mid-
January 1996)*

SHEVA: That song is dedicated to my lovely angel, Eti.

(*Spot fades as* SHEVA *blows a kiss out to the audience.)*

Scene Two

*(A government sponsored party in Jerusalem at the Hotel
King David. Applause from Scene One dove-tails into this
scene.* SHEVA's *singing is heard ever so faintly.)*

EZRA: I'm working on my English.

SONYA: Be my guest.

EZRA: This is a banquet that spares no expense.

SONYA: It most certainly is.

EZRA: And so many well dressed Americans here. The
food is very good.

SONYA: But of course.

EZRA: Except for the egg rolls. Nearly fossilized. Who
the hell ordered egg rolls?

(SONYA *laughs.)*

EZRA: What's the occasion?

SONYA: A circumcision for a late arrival?

EZRA: Circumcision, yes. Your English is far better than your Hebrew.

SONYA: Bullshit.

EZRA: I adore you, dear Sonya Gelman. Russia's foremost linguist. You link the great incontinents together.

SONYA: Continents.

EZRA: These strange words simply fall off your beautiful tongue.

SONYA: An adopted language has profound...

EZRA/SONYA: Misery. Mystery

SONYA: Your English is as bad as...

EZRA: My Hebrew? *(Pause)* Look at the beautiful flowers.

SONYA: Colors of the rainbow.

EZRA: You can smell air conditioned Paradise. Shut your pretty eyes please.

SONYA: I never shut my eyes, Ezra, in the company of unmarried men. I am not a fool.

EZRA: *(Shuts his eyes)* I am. My heart is full.

SONYA: And my stomach is empty.

EZRA: The Jerusalem cooks put hummus into nearly every dish. What is the meaning of this?

SONYA: An absurd abundance of Garbanzo beans. Wretched gas for the Greenhouse Effect. You'll find half the new buildings use hummus due to the cement shortage. Will these buildings stand after thirty years?

EZRA: Undoubtedly, I won't. Weak prostate.

SONYA: Quit drinking before noon.

(EZRA winces.)

SONYA: Did you give blood this week?

EZRA: I didn't.

SONYA: The country's seriously low.

EZRA: Well, I have a low platelet count.

SONYA: I gave two pints. A successful blood drive.

EZRA: Mazel tov. I drink two pints.

SONYA: You're putting on weight, my old man.

EZRA: Yes, well, martinis with lunch improves my memory. Are you expecting the filthy rich American talent scout?

SONYA: Which filthy rich American scout?

EZRA: Fishman, the sports czar. Sharansky's pal. He's recruiting for his spanking new soccer team.

SONYA: Don't screw with me, darling. Americans don't play soccer.

EZRA: Now they do. Don't you read Newsweek? *(Pause)* You just won't tell me, Sonya. We are terrible friends.

SONYA: We are not terrible friends.

EZRA: What the hell are we then?

SONYA: Political refugees that shared a corner hotel room once.

(EZRA laughs despite himself.)

SONYA: I was too clumsy, yes?

EZRA: Where is your charismatic husband?

SONYA: I don't know.

EZRA: Still married to this jerk?

SONYA: No. Yes. Somewhere in between.

EZRA: You know I'm working on another project.

SONYA: I know.

EZRA: You don't approve?

SONYA: The next group flying in is not Jewish, Ezra. I read the e-mail.

EZRA: Whose e-mail?

SONYA: I can't say.

EZRA: It's true, yes. This is a humanitarian effort.

SONYA: This is crap.

EZRA: Well...

SONYA: Something you want?

EZRA: Are you asking or telling me?

SONYA: I'm asking you.

EZRA: You know my answer.

SONYA: You're a very complex person.

EZRA: Is it my cologne?

SONYA: No.

EZRA: My loud reputation?

SONYA: What reputation?

EZRA: A desert Ethiopian from my ass to my elbows. The Jewish Lawrence of Arabia with fallen arches.

SONYA: And I'm the incomparable Queen of Sheba who can kill you with two fingers.

EZRA: Kill me in bed, cupcake. *(Pause)* Who is this singer?

SONYA: Isn't she one of your girls?

(EZRA *nods his head, feigning bewilderment.*)

SONYA: This crop of African immigrants is wildly evangelistic.

EZRA: They're persecuted Jews with crosses stamped on their foreheads.

SONYA: So much for The Law of Return for real Jews.

EZRA: Who the hell is real these days? Madonna studying Kabbalah?

SONYA: I like Madonna.

EZRA: And for years Sammy Davis thought he was a New York Jew trapped in Las Vegas.

SONYA: The Falas Mura have no intention of converting.

EZRA: Open your heart. Give them time in Absorption. They are my cousins.

SONYA: Darling, your "cousins" love Jesus and will go around knocking on everyone's damn door.

EZRA: *(Distracted)* Oh Christ, Ariel Sharon is walking in. Fat as ever. Atilla the Jew.

SONYA: Where is your new money coming from?

EZRA: *(Attention returns)* What?

SONYA: The new, clean money. The countable money. Your *legal* money.

EZRA: United Jewish Appeal and the arrogant Canadian Jew who runs the Seagram Corporation.

SONYA: *(Sweetly)* I don't believe you.

EZRA: What? You think the government is throwing shekels at us?

SONYA: When you lie, Ezra, you're eyebrows knit a little twisted X right here. *(Touches him)* I need your full support with the Knesset vote.

EZRA: Your happy Russians have enough duty-free vodka until the Messiah, Sonya. One third of the men are drunk and another third are in an illegal racket. Our problems are not equal.

SONYA: Government funds were earmarked for Russian Jews.

EZRA: Where's Sharansky? I want to talk to Sharansky, damnit.

SONYA: *(Persistent)* And you have Barbara Steisand performing a Tel Aviv benefit for the Falasha.

EZRA: We don't call ourselves Falasha, Sonya.

SONYA: Who will sing for the cold refugees from Minsk?

EZRA: Neil Diamond.

SONYA: What are you going to say to Sharansky?

EZRA: I'll ask the Minister if he's been to Ethiopia's capital—Addis Ababa. But we know the answer— *Tenastyllin. Salam. Indemina? Dana. (Sardonic)* "Hello. Shalom. How are you? I'm just wonderful, thanks."

SONYA: He'll say, "Falas Mura. Christian inside and out".

EZRA: What makes this wounded Ethiopian tribe the enemy of Israel?

SONYA: For one, you can't have a nation of false Jews.

EZRA: Some would say we already have that.

SONYA: This is too small a country and every immigrant Jew is struggling. *(Pause)* Ezra, there can be no more airlifts. Wake up! You're monopolizing all the vacant shelters.

EZRA: Last month you said you would lend support. Are these mood swings?

SONYA: *(Demurely)* I changed my mind after a talk with the Prime Minister. If you engineer an airlift without his blessings, you embarrass everyone and I'll catch hell from my Russian refugees.

EZRA: Your people can't blame you.

SONYA: My job will be a thousand times harder. Work with these limitations. Just like sweet Moses.

EZRA: Moses was black.

SONYA: You have a photograph maybe?

EZRA: Yes, in my wallet. You never know.

SONYA: Spectacular.

EZRA: The color of a Jew's skin is that of God's heart.

(Faint applause after a song)

EZRA: But unfortunately God has no color.

SONYA: Or no heart?

(End of scene)

Scene Three

(Jerusalem diamond cutting store, back room. mid- January)

HESHI: Wash your hands.

ETI: I did.

HESHI: Show me.

(ETI does.)

HESHI: Sit down. Not there, over here.

(ETI finds the second chair and sits.)

HESHI: We have two hours. O K?

ETI: *(Respectful and playful)* O K, boss.

HESHI: Don't call me that.

ETI: *(Smiling generously)* Mister Heshi? Hello, Mister Heshi? *(Sings a little ditty)*

He gives me diamonds, he gives me pearls.
He gives me felafel, he likes my curls.
Mister mister mister mister mister Heshi!

HESHI: No singing.

(ETI *continues humming.*)

HESHI: And don't call me Heshi. Mister Lebowitz. Say it, Eti.

ETI: Mister Heshi is sweeter.

HESHI: I make you my student.

ETI: It is my honor.

HESHI: I know you have brains and some gifts.

ETI: *(With warm mischief)* I'm a singer. I'm a lover. That you know.

HESHI: *(Laughs in spite of himself)* I'll bet. Time will tell. And comes to you. All in good time. And so will the young girls. You have good looks, boychik. Clean ebony skin, sharp eyes and graceful hands.

ETI: Thank you. I like your beard. So teach me.

HESHI: A diamond will always seek a Jew. And a Jew will always find a diamond. The first law of science. When a Jew is forced from a country, he takes what he can carry. A fistful of diamonds. For he cannot take his house, his cattle, his furniture or even his bank account. A fistful of diamonds, Eti. Nothing more.

ETI: My brothers and I came with a bag of clothes. We left a wood hut and five goats.

HESHI: I'm sorry for you and your family. *(Softly)* Are you a pious Jew like me?

ETI: I am, sir. And I fear God like you.

HESHI: You pray in the morning and in the evening?

ETI: I do. In my own way. *(Hums a melody again)*

HESHI: Maybe you are more pious than me?

ETI: Only God knows such things.

HESHI: *(Dryly amused)* God knows us better than we know ourselves. You make me laugh inside. *(Pause)* There are the four "C's to each diamond. Clarity. Color. Cut.

ETI: Coupon?

HESHI: And Carat. There is a rating system. Color can go from "D" to "G, H, I, J" all the way to "Z". Most appraisers will agree on set principles. And, of course, most jewelers are shrewd to sell diamonds which fool the public. I am not one of them. I am Mister Honesty. Do you understand that?

ETI: Yes, I do, Mister Honesty Lebowitz.

HESHI: I'm not a crazy man.

ETI: No, sir, not crazy at all.

HESHI: We live to make some profit, or we drop dead. You would die in Ethiopia. You will thrive in Jerusalem. *(Pause)* This is why you must know your alphabet. What town are you from?

ETI: Addis Ababa. The capital.

HESHI: Your sponsor told me it was Quara.

ETI: Yes, Quara is the outskirts of the Addis Ababa.

HESHI: Five hundred miles on the outskirts? You still have family there?

ETI: *(Flustered)* No.

HESHI: I know more than you think I know.

ETI: People in Quara are very unlucky. Many never made it on the list to go.

HESHI: How did you get on the list?

ETI: I don't know, sir.

HESHI: Your father paid someone.

ETI: No.

HESHI: That's how it goes, Eti.

ETI: Sir.

HESHI: Someone got paid.

ETI: Maybe. I was younger then. It wasn't easy to leave the land.

HESHI: But you'll never return to Ethiopia.

ETI: I don't want my family to suffer.

HESHI: I understand.

ETI: I don't know if God hears my prayers.

HESHI: God does. My brother's wife is from Yemen.

ETI: Yemen is not Ethiopia.

HESHI: Shaaa! She's not as dark as you. But your smile is nicer. I don't know why he married her. I don't know why she married him. A rocky marriage. She will never return to Yemen. Her life hangs on a thread. Those are her words. *(Pause)* You will learn how to polish my cheaper diamonds, Eti. That is all you will do. Along the way, maybe in a year I will give you other tasks. We'll see. Cutting diamonds is a master art. I am a master. It could make you rich or make you a soul of greed. I fight my own greed. I am not a perfect man. *(Pause)* And you are not perfect. I'll watch you like a hawk. I can see with an eye behind my head. That's right. I have a small insurance policy and two hand guns. I carry one. I hide the other. And I can be more avenging than the Almighty. No matter what favor I owe you. *(Pause)* When my wife comes to the store, you must ignore her. I do. Make no exceptions.

ETI: Yes, Mister Lebowitz.

HESHI: When she offers you her rancid food or some deadly bricks that she baked, just smile and say "no thank you, Mrs Lebowitz.". Hunger has its limits. Eat your meals at home. My wife has other virtues. *(Pause)* And when you marry, pick a woman who complains less than her mother and who will not imitate your own mother. I say this to be charitable. O K?

ETI: O K.

HESHI: You have a girlfriend?

ETI: I did.

HESHI: Oh?

ETI: She trashed me. She's a club singer.

HESHI: A club singer? Who needs aggravation? Better to be free, boychik. You can dance with another pretty girl now. *(Pause)* The phone machine is on. We won't be disturbed. Why do you blink so much?

ETI: An illness five years ago.

HESHI: Close your eye. Now look at my finger. *(Pause)* That eye is a lazy eye.

ETI: I know, sir.

HESHI: *(Flashing a finger in front of that eye)* Not blind in that eye?

ETI: I can see everything from both eyes in good light..

HESHI: *(Sensing the lie, under his breath)* Oy...vey iz meir! I know about the Falas Mura.

ETI: I'm not Falas Mura. I am all Jewish, only Jewish. Not one finger is Jesus.

HESHI: Never say that name inside my shop. O K?

ETI: O K.

HESHI: Kiss the Mezuzah on the door when you enter and when you leave. *(Pause. Pronouncing "polish" like the nation)* It's time to polish.

ETI: *(Echoing* HESHI*)* Polish.

HESHI: *(No real distinction as* HESHI *says the word)* Not Pole-ish. Poll-ish.

ETI: *(Echoing again)* Polish. Thank you.

HESHI: For what?

ETI: For helping.

HESHI: I'm a businessman. I'll profit by your labor.

ETI: Before my father died, he told me what he wanted. A fair chance at success.

HESHI: I see.

ETI: And my mother echoed my father.

HESHI: Where is she?

ETI: *(Lying)* In Quara. But the Jewish Agency has her file. That will take forever.

HESHI: Still, you don't want to be an orphan in Jerusalem.

*(*ETI *shakes his head yes)*

HESHI: God willing.

ETI: I need to find a living angel. This is a fact, Mr. Lebowitz. I want success denied to my father. If not in the sports stadium, then in the diamond district. I will pole-ish your stones.

(End of scene)

Scene Four

(Restaurant. January)

EZRA: A lovely meal.

FISHMAN: *(Picks up the check)* No, I insist. It was my invitation.

EZRA: Thank you.

FISHMAN: Can I drive you somewhere?

EZRA: Paris? *(Smiles)*

FISHMAN: If your nephew is all that you say he is, I'll owe you big time.

EZRA: He's a bolt of lightning, as fast as Ethiopia's Olympic Deratu Tulu.

FISHMAN: Ezra, you must be very proud of him.

EZRA: *(Nodding)* I must thank Ronit Melkav at the university for arranging this.

FISHMAN: I've been on the prowl for some time. Israelis love to cash in on professional sports. Why is he so hard to find?

EZRA: Eti's restless. After army service, college didn't agree with him. Some days he loves to play sports. Other days he's depressed. Ongoing struggles with his mother. As I said over the phone, I'll help recruit him every step to a secure contract.

FISHMAN: And, of course, you'll earn a nice bonus once he signs.

EZRA: Skip that, Mr. Fishman, and do something special.

FISHMAN: I give every year to the Jewish Agency.

EZRA: Splendid. But I'm involved in a dear mission involving the last airlifts.

FISHMAN: I know.

EZRA: *(Insistent)* No, you don't know. There are thousands of bereft Ethiopians with Jewish blood in their veins.

FISHMAN: I see.

EZRA: You don't have to pay me a thing and you don't need to overpay my nephew. Instead, direct your generosity towards the last Ethiopians—the Falas Mura.

FISHMAN: How much?

EZRA: As much as you can afford and I want you to use your good graces with the Prime Minister's cabinet.

FISHMAN: Ezra...

EZRA: I know how influential you are. You helped pay the way for Minister Sharansky to leave Russia.

FISHMAN: You're way off base. Besides, I can only support bona fide Jews. Not the bottom of the barrel. You know there can be no more airlifts. The last official migration ended with Operation Solomon.

EZRA: Many of Israel's renowned operations were unofficial.

FISHMAN: *(Sarcastic)* Really?

EZRA: Let me relate a story about Solomon and the Queen of Sheba.

FISHMAN: *(Glances at watch)* I'm running late.

EZRA: Sit, my friend. *(Reaches for FISHMAN's arm)* King Solomon needed Sheba's trade routes while she craved his Mediterranean seaports. He fell deeply in love and agreed to give her a child. That child became...

FISHMAN: *(Impatient)* Your blessed Falasha.

EZRA: The celebrated lost tribe of Israel.

FISHMAN: The black Jew on Ethiopia Street.

EZRA: And Solomon heard a bird say that Sheba worshiped the sun. So he sent a message: "There is but one God invisible." Sheba came to his court to argue but the King's angels warned him that the Queen had animal legs under her gown.

FISHMAN: I've known many women with such legs. *(Rising)*

EZRA: Solomon's engineers built a glass floor, but he was reluctant to look up.

FISHMAN: Just find me your nephew, O K?

EZRA: In this instance, don't be like Solomon, Mister Fishman.

(EZRA reaches to shake FISHMAN's hand)

FISHMAN: I respect you Ezra. We worship the same God, but you're gambling heavily on these Ethiopians who don't even know three things about Judaism. I'll try to do what I can when the time arrives.

EZRA: Thank you.

FISHMAN: *(Breaking from his grasp)* I really have to be going.

(End of scene)

Scene Five

(Ethiopian apartment complex just outside of Jerusalem. mid-January. RONIT translates several Hebrew phrases.)

RONIT: *Ish hasakim hashir mamerica. (Yes, this is the wealthy business man from America).*

DELAL: *(Bluntly) Hanaliem shalo mahoarot. Haim hoo sohan mmshlti?*

RONIT: She says your shoes are ugly.

FISHMAN: I like my shoes.

RONIT: She thinks you're a government agent.

FISHMAN: *(Laughing)* No, I'm not a government spy.

DELAL: You are.

RONIT: You don't need me. Delal can speak to you directly.

FISHMAN: My dear woman...I make too much money to be a spy. Tell her, Ronit.

RONIT: Mister Fishman is a private citizen from the United States.

FISHMAN: I also have a delightful home in Tel Aviv.

RONIT: Homes in several countries.

DELAL: What do you want?

FISHMAN: To make your family happy and wealthy.

RONIT: You look ill, Delal. Are you all right? Atha margish tov?

DELAL: I have a fever.

RONIT: Mister Fishman, another time would be better.

FISHMAN: I'll miss my plane. Ezra promised.

DELAL: What do you want? My husband's dead.

FISHMAN: Delal, I love the old Ethiopia Street. No place like it in all of Jerusalem. That beautiful Coptic church. So much history. I believe in the expanding Ethiopian Jewish community. And I am absolutely stunned by the physical talents of Ethiopia's golden children. Israel is stronger because you are here.

RONIT: *Hoo maariss at hakehila hatiopit vomer Israel hazaka ki atem kan (He admires the Ethiopian community and says Israel is stronger because you are here).*

FISHMAN: I'm also a good friend of your brother-in-law Ezra.

RONIT: *Hoo haver tov shel hagiss shelha (He is a good friend of your brother-in-law).*

DELAL: Ezra has too many friends.

FISHMAN: Yes, well, he told me to seek out your extremely gifted young son.

DELAL: Which one?

FISHMAN: Your youngest and brightest. The runner. The amazing athlete.

RONIT: Delal, he wants your Eti—for professional sports in America.

DELAL: Eti?

RONIT: *Ze hakasef bbank.* This is money in the bank.

FISHMAN: A lot of money, Delal, and a world of prestige. Where is your boy?

DELAL: He left the army.

FISHMAN: I know that, dear. That was many many months ago.

DELAL: He hates the army. He cannot kill. He is pious Jew.

RONIT: Do you want him to go back to college?

DELAL: Yes. And married.

RONIT: Mister Fishman respects a college education.

DELAL: Where is my brother-in-law?

FISHMAN: Ezra left the country for a few days. He went to Ethiopia. Addis Ababa.

DELAL: I want my son to marry. All my children are married.

RONIT: Where is Eti?

DELAL: With his wild girl friend.

FISHMAN: *(To* RONIT*)* I spoke with the girl. She sings in small night clubs. They had a fight.

RONIT: A bad fight?

FISHMAN: The police came.

(FISHMAN *and* RONIT *both throw a look at* DELAL.)

DELAL: *Rak lo meshtara (God forbid not the police).* The police don't want Eti. No, no, he is good son. Will visit before Passover.

RONIT: She doesn't know his whereabouts.

FISHMAN: I see.

(DELAL *wanders off.*)

FISHMAN: Thank you, Delal. *(Quiet, wry voice to* RONIT*)* Do we wait until Passover for him?

RONIT: He'll turn up in the neighborhood. Give it a week. I'll get this all arranged.

FISHMAN: I like your motivation, Ronit.

RONIT: My brother runs an absorption center. It's abysmal. No hot water. Holes in the roof.

FISHMAN: A shame. I'm good for a big pledge. I'll call your brother.

RONIT: We'll probably find the boy as soon as you write the check.

FISHMAN: Everyone along this chain wants a check.

RONIT: That's the definition of Jewish enterprise, Mister Fishman. We'll find him before Sunday.

FISHMAN: Do you feel that lucky?

RONIT: I had a good dialogue with Eti while he was on my campus.

FISHMAN: Do you always court wealthy Americans for your campus fund drive? *(He exaggerates a smile. Pause)* Is he an observant Jew?

RONIT: You saw the Star of David on Delal's bureau. Is it an issue?

FISHMAN: The press calls Falas Mura many awful names. He might be here illegally.

RONIT: Falasha and Falas Mura are equally misunderstood. If you're persecuted by gentiles in the Diaspora, you might as well be a Jew.

FISHMAN: My cousin works under the Prime Minister. In unofficial cabinet meetings some call them—Sheba's little bastards.

RONIT: Name calling is a modern evil

FISHMAN: Indeed. *(Pause)* I'll give you three days to find the boy.

(End of scene)

Scene Six

(A Jerusalem street café. Mid-January)

SHEVA: You're late.

ETI: I know.

SHEVA: But you're not sorry.

ETI: I'm sorry, Sheva.

SHEVA: You could have called.

ETI: I hate the phone.

SHEVA: That's wonderful.

ETI: You sing here tonight.

SHEVA: Every Wednesday. With my crazy band.

ETI: Are you hungry?

SHEVA: A little.

ETI: I'm starved.

SHEVA: Where were you?

ETI: Kept late at the diamond shop.

SHEVA: He gave you work?

ETI: Yeah.

SHEVA: I don't believe it.

ETI: Because he's Ashkanazim?

SHEVA: That's right.

ETI: I saved his life last month.

SHEVA: What?

ETI: I walked into a robbery in Old Jerusalem. Late at night. I chased the thief away. Lebowitz owns my cousins' building. Charges them like it's a five star hotel.

SHEVA: So Lebowitz's letting you sweep the floor?

ETI: I'm apprenticing.

SHEVA: He asked if you were circumcised?

ETI: Not yet.

SHEVA: *(Laughs and pokes him below the belt)* He will. And then check you with a jeweler's lens. These puffed up European Jews! *(Pause)* Stupid, Eti. My beautiful, lovely boy. Track star and village idiot. You wear two crowns and you quit school for this honor?

ETI: I missed too many classes. *(Pause)* Why are you so angry?

SHEVA: Because I want something.

ETI: What?

SHEVA: I want to run away.

ETI: Where?

SHEVA: Anywhere from Israel with a resort hotel and dance floor.

ETI: Inside you're not Jewish.

SHEVA: More Jewish than you. And more pious.

ETI: Prove it.

SHEVA: I know how to shop for bargains and how to talk to God. *(Sneaks a kiss)*

ETI: I have important things to do.

SHEVA: So you can't run away today with me?

ETI: I have no money.

SHEVA: You have the fastest feet in Jerusalem. That's better than gold.

ETI: And you have the fastest mouth.

SHEVA: If not the fastest, at least the prettiest. *(Pause)* An American clown was looking for you yesterday. Expensive clothes, gold bracelet. And a red nose.

ETI: He came to you?

SHEVA: Everyone comes to me. I'm a lounge act in a skinny dress. Exotic singer for hire. *(Pause)* I said nothing.

ETI: What did he want?

SHEVA: Your goddamn legs. His name is Fishman and he wants to sign a contract.

ETI: You're lying.

SHEVA: Why would I lie, Eti? He gave me his business card. *(Producing the card)* He was with Ronit Melkav, from the university. Is that the woman that kicked you out?

ETI: No, Ronit helped me with medical excuses.

SHEVA: Let's run away.

ETI: *(Grabs the card playfully)* No, I have to call him! This is my ticket.

SHEVA: Don't grab. Bad manners.

ETI: Thanks, Sheva.

SHEVA: Say it from your heart.

ETI: I thank you for everything good.

SHEVA: Are you tomorrow's soccer star?

ETI: I could be.

SHEVA: Or our next Olympic runner? And so tough on your poor mother. *(Pause)* The Russian boys from the projects are still following me.

ETI: Don't walk by their street.

SHEVA: They know where I live.

ETI: It's the way you dress.

SHEVA: *(Teasing)* Or the way I walk? Maybe they come to the club to hear me sing. I can't stop that, but I feel eyes on my back in the alleys. *(Pause)* We both want success yet you're...

ETI: I'm not afraid of anything.

SHEVA: You're afraid of me.

(SHEVA kisses ETI as he flinches.)

SHEVA: Afraid of army service. Afraid of doctor exams.

ETI: I gave to the blood drive.

SHEVA: Did it hurt?

ETI: No. Two minutes with an ugly nurse.

SHEVA: I'll donate this week. At my school you get a free movie pass or pair of sunglasses.

ETI: *(Teasing)* So you don't want to run away today?

SHEVA: I do with your money. We could get to Greece in a day.

ETI: Greece?

SHEVA: You want to fight over Greece?

ETI: When we fight, you call the police.

SHEVA: Then we should never fight about Greece.

ETI: Why do you stay with me, Sheva? I have no money now.

SHEVA: I like the way you kiss. And you'll be rich and famous one day.

ETI: Which reason is more important?

(SHEVA *smiles.*)

SHEVA: Kissing is always more important. (*In a low voice, she starts to sing a song while caressing his face.*)

(*End of scene*)

Scene Seven

(RONIT's *college office. Mid-January*)

EZRA: I was curious about this semester's testing.

RONIT: The results look promising.

EZRA: And the Ethiopian students?

RONIT: You worry too much.

EZRA: My only pleasure in life, Ronit.

RONIT: Funding will continue for each Ethiopian student.

EZRA: I don't want to see all these kids turn into farm laborers.

RONIT: Some will, despite college.

EZRA: How long have you worked at this college?

RONIT: (*Sarcasm*) Sixty years. I've seen "generations" of Ethiopians. Beginning with Operation Moses '84 airlift.

EZRA: You directed more funds to the Ethiopian students.

RONIT: Only angels do such stunts.

EZRA: And you've been very good to my nephew.

RONIT: I like Eti. He has the makings of a great athlete. I have a good hunch about him. And I know Fishman's money and connections are good.

EZRA: Let's hope so.

RONIT: I heard a rumor about a secret airlift...the end of April.

EZRA: I can't comment, Ronit.

(RONIT *glares at* EZRA.)

EZRA: Is it a mistake to have twenty thousand additional Ethiopians drop out of the sky?

RONIT: Certainly a remarkable image, Ezra.

EZRA: Do you know how many Ethiopians are in the Knesset?

RONIT: One?

EZRA: While there are three elected Israeli Arabs in the Knesset.

RONIT: As with anything political, you start with one.

EZRA: Ronit, what would you do if you sat on the hat of the Chief Rabbinate?

RONIT: I would die of shame.

EZRA: And I would laugh. The airlift is scheduled for two weeks. It can't wait until April. Cargo planes are hard to hijack. No one knows the timetable. Not even the Ministry. I got to get to Sharanksy.

RONIT: You were one of the first Ethiopian officers in the Air Force. Certainly you have some clout.

EZRA: An intimate connection is needed.

RONIT: You're the mastermind behind this airlift, aren't you?

EZRA: *(Covering poorly)* No.

RONIT: *(Smiles sadly)* If you bring more black Christians, you only hurt black Jews already settled.

EZRA: They share the same ancestry. We can prove it.

RONIT: D N A? Photos? Shared memories of massacres?

EZRA: Rally the college for me.

RONIT: And then a Nobel Peace Prize?

EZRA: After this last airlift, I just want to pass a kidney stone.

RONIT: Passing a kidney stone is easier. Get some sleep, Ezra. You look exhausted.

EZRA: Do I? *(Pause)* What's really happening with Eti?

RONIT: Your nephew had too many absences. He has some eye trouble. It was his decision to leave.

EZRA: You do keep tabs on him, Ronit?

RONIT: *(Hands his a scrap of paper)* You might find him with his girlfriend. She's a handful for the entire Israeli army.

(End of scene)

Scene Eight

(DELAL's home. February)

SHEVA: I made him come back. Eti doesn't trust any woman. Always testing me, Mrs Shlomo. He wants us to get married but he won't say when. What's a girl to do? Wait for Santa Claus?
Eti's working for a fat white diamond merchant? Look at him. Silent like a stone. When he talks to my family,

he whispers. From his mouth they can't understand
anything. But they like his smile. Want him to be
my husband. I love him. I made him come back to
you. Mend his clothes. I cook for him. Sing to him. I
understand him in a deep way. I do.

DELAL: Eti?

ETI: What?

DELAL: Look at your hands.

ETI: What?

DELAL: Wash.

ETI: I brought you some money, Ima.

DELAL: Wash your hands.

ETI: You look sick.

DELAL: Wash your hands. *(To* SHEVA*)* You too.

ETI: Ima. Not enough goods in the kitchen.

DELAL: I make do.

ETI: We can't stay.

DELAL: Food on the table. Sit and eat.

ETI: Not hungry.

DELAL: *(Looking at* SHEVA*)* She's hungry. Sit. And eat.
I cooked all day. *(Brings a large bowl of water to* ETI*)*
Where are you living?

ETI: In town.

DELAL: With her?

SHEVA: No. I live with my family. My parents would
like to meet you. *(Pause)* Maybe things will change.
Yes?

DELAL: Sheva.

SHEVA: What?

DELAL: You talk too much.

SHEVA: I can sing for you?

DELAL: Stop talking.

(Hands ETI *a towel. He puts his hand in the bowl.)*

*(*SHEVA *hums a melody softly.)*

ETI: She has a voice, Ima.

DELAL: Why a diamond merchant?

ETI: I like diamonds.

DELAL: Diamonds bring misery.

*(*SHEVA *washes hands and sits.)*

ETI: I'll get your diamond earrings and rings soon. The food smells good. You should open a restaurant. "DELAL'S ETHIOPIA."

DELAL: Your father says don't work for a diamond merchant..

ETI: *(Sweetly)* Father is dead. How can he speak?

DELAL: He speaks to me.

ETI: I hear him then.

DELAL: Don't be a stranger to this house. You could stay in school.

ETI: Let's talk about this later.

DELAL: Sit.

*(*ETI *sits.)*

DELAL: I go to the doctor's clinic. I learn a little each day. You have to learn very fast here. I can read a face faster than you can a book. *(Pause)* When Eti was a boy, he made us laugh. The youngest child has such talent. Now his talent is running because he is running away. *(To* SHEVA*)* What does he want to say?

SHEVA: I don't know.

ETI: I think Santa Claus is Jewish. When you fly in a bright red suit, you must be Jewish to survive. Santa should visit every black Jewish home.

(SHEVA *laughs*)

ETI: My mother is not laughing.

DELAL: (*Strained smile*) No.

ETI: (*Sweet teasing*) Why cry?

DELAL: Your brothers are more sincere.

ETI: You wouldn't like me if I were that sincere, Ima. (*Puts napkin over himself like an Arab headdress and affects an Arab dialect*) "Now I am very sincere. My name is Omar and you get no oil until you kiss me."

(SHEVA *laughs.* DELAL *pulls the napkin from* ETI's *head.*)

ETI: I'm taking all my clothes and things, Ima.

DELAL: Ask your father.

SHEVA: Your son will be an Israeli hero. Be rich and smart. The best athlete.

DELAL: I don't care.

SHEVA: Tell him that he can do this.

DELAL: He does not believe with his heart in God.

ETI: I believe in God.

DELAL: God doesn't believe you, Eti.

ETI: God was in my dreams. Told me to go for the American offer so I can buy you a house, Ima.

DELAL: More a boy than a man, Eti. (*Long look at* SHEVA) She wants to say something.

ETI: Sheva said enough.

DELAL: (*Behind* ETI, *her hands on his shoulders*) Speak.

SHEVA: I'm pregnant.

(ETI *is surprised*)

SHEVA: It's true, Eti. I saw a doctor yesterday.

ETI: *(Trying to placate his mother)* Ima...

SHEVA: I love your son. Please accept me, Mrs. Shlomo. We have a beautiful future.

(DELAL *picks up the water bowl and walks away slowly*)

(End of scene)

Scene Nine

(Diamond shop. February. ETI *is showing* HESHI *photos from his college athletic races)*

ETI: I broke the school's record by a ten seconds.

HESHI: I see.

ETI: This was in the newspaper last year.

HESHI: *(Distracted)* Very nice.

ETI: My coach said I was the fastest in Jerusalem.

HESHI: I have something to ask you. *(Stacks photos together)* This is very awkward, Eti. I'm missing a key to the back room.

ETI: I don't have it, Mister Lebowitz.

HESHI: You haven't seen keys at all?

ETI: No.

HESHI: Do you think I simply lost it?

ETI: I don't know, Mister Lebowitz.

HESHI: Do I look like a fool? I like you. You know that. *(Pause)* Empty your pockets, Eti. *(Silence)* You heard me. Please empty them.

(ETI *obliges. Some coins, a pocket knife, his keys)*

HESHI: Put everything on the counter.

(ETI *does so.*)

HESHI: Those are not my keys?

ETI: No.

HESHI: *(Picks up* ETI's *keys)* These are not my keys.

ETI: Maybe your wife? I've seen her with keys before, sir.

HESHI: Now I have to change the locks. Eti, there are days when I don't trust you. I don't know why that is. Sometimes it's how fast you move your hands.

ETI: I'm going to be a father, Mister Lebowitz.

HESHI: *(Hurt)* We have to trust each other. You showed me your school awards.

ETI: Sports can be just a dream. I'll have a real trade in gems. I don't want to be naive.

HESHI: All Ethiopians are. You give blood and the government throws it in the gutter.

How naive is that? Are you going to marry her?

ETI: I have to. It's what I feel each night.

HESHI: Have you asked her? She may turn you down.

ETI: I don't think so.

HESHI: I want to meet her.

ETI: Why?

HESHI: You need my approval for all the things you do.

ETI: She thinks your people look down on us.

HESHI: God knows that's not true. You bring her here tomorrow, Eti.

(End of scene)

Scene Ten

(Hotel lobby. February)

SONYA: It's gotten very bad.

EZRA: For whom?

SONYA: For you, for me, Moishe Pipik, for all strangers in this hallowed land.

EZRA: More Russian than Israeli, Sonya?

SONYA: I don't know. Just a middle aged women.

EZRA: Sometimes I feel very strange here. Do you like this hotel?

SONYA: The bidets are brand new.

EZRA: Why did you give up your apartment?

SONYA: My marriage is failing. But you're not coming upstairs tonight, even though you're wearing your lucky jacket.

EZRA: My district is boiling over. All due to the wasted Ethiopian blood.

SONYA: The mayor should be shot.

EZRA: It's not just this city, Sonya.

SONYA: There's fear of an AIDS epidemic. Statistics about Africa.

EZRA: My people were encouraged to give blood. There were signs everywhere. Radios spots. Leaflets. We feel like a leper colony.

SONYA: That doesn't make you want to return to Ethiopia. *(Pause)* Don't look at me that way.

EZRA: I found a donor who will finance half of the airlift.

SONYA: Who?

EZRA: I can't say. So now I need a favor from you.

SONYA: *(These two lines overlap)* You want me to speak to the Ministers.

EZRA: Sharansky, your old Russian pal.

SONYA: Don't press me, Ezra.

EZRA: This is a perfect time. The Prime Minister has to show leniency after this blood scandal. A half fueled cargo plane will force a landing.

SONYA: *(Knowing where this is going)* Ezra!

EZRA: *(Next two lines overlap)* And it should come from you.

SONYA: You're dreaming the impossible.

EZRA: A tribute to the little Ethiopia Street of . yesteryear.

SONYA: You've lost touch with reality.

EZRA: Christians Ethiopians believe the Jews among them are sorcerers and transform at night into hyenas.

SONYA: What if you botch this airlift?

EZRA: I can't think like that.

SONYA: The Cabinet Ministers will ask the same question. Certainly Sharansky will.

EZRA: I know we have a major conflict between our wards. It comes down to housing allocation, not jet landing rights. Let my people come, Sonya.

SONYA: In my "Yud" neighborhood, Zvi Ben-Ari hired a Swiss pilot to smuggle him out of a Zurich prison to come here. Merchants fear him. The police do nothing. Politicians are on his payroll. This Russian doesn't deserve citizenship. Fake Jews like Ben-Ari slip past us.

EZRA: I'm only asking for two thousand housing units from your wards.

SONYA: You're really out of your mind! How do you expect me to pacify Russians crowded into two room apartments?

EZRA: Sonya, you could convince Yasir Arafat to shave. Russians have professional skills to adapt. A quarter of them are not even Jewish.

SONYA: I need to think it over.

EZRA: Tell me in the morning.

SONYA: I promise nothing.

EZRA: I understand what intimacy is with you.

SONYA: Ezra. You're impossible! *(Pause)* I want to leave Israel. I want to live in a place where I can just take care of myself. *(She rises and stares at him.)* Are you going to call in the morning?

EZRA: I'm sorry about your marriage. *(He rises.)*

SONYA: No, you're not. It's the furthest thing from your mind.

EZRA: He's a putz. You married a shit. I feel for you. Have dinner with me tonight.

SONYA: Nothing more than dinner.

EZRA: A beautiful smile, Sonya. May I say that?

(SONYA smiles weakly and EZRA squeezes her chin.)

EZRA: May I, Sonya, may I?

(End of scene)

Scene Eleven

(DELAL's home. February)

ETI: What time is he coming?

DELAL: Three o'clock. He's coming with your uncle.

ETI: What happens when his doctors examine me?.

DELAL: Trust your uncle.

ETI: But it's my eyes, Ima. The army doctor said things to me.

DELAL: What did he say?

ETI: Retinis pigmentosa. Surgery can't fix everything. Now my eye hurts more. After I left home. Maybe I run too hard and I pay with my sight. When I'm tired I see shadows and color.

Close up I see a little better. At night it's hard. In a couple of years something could happen to the good eye.

DELAL: I'm sorry, Eti.

ETI: If I lie to others about this, God will know. And then I will certainly lose my eyes.

DELAL: I will make your decisions for you.

ETI: If I get paid big money to play soccer, demons may come for my eyes.

DELAL: These demons are not from Quara.

ETI: It doesn't matter where they are from.

DELAL: If you ask God to help...

ETI: How if I cheat others?

DELAL: Is this why you got this girl pregnant?

ETI: Blame her perfume, not me. The army doctor said that my eyes are like father's.

And his eyes failed after the famine.

DELAL: Yes, Eti.

ETI: You insulted God, didn't you Ima?

DELAL: Don't talk like that.

ETI: You blamed God for our misery before we came to Jerusalem. Here our family is not Jewish enough. You think that annoys God. You can't speak Hebrew like the chosen.

DELAL: No.

ETI: And you think God hates that I run faster than the white boys.

DELAL: No.

ETI: Then why do you blame God every time I see you?

DELAL: I do not.

ETI: You blame me for being an athlete.

DELAL: Why fool around with Sheva girl?

ETI: She's no girl.

DELAL: I see no modesty.

ETI: You dropped father in Quara like old luggage.

DELAL: *(Slaps him)* How dare you...

ETI: It's true.

DELAL: He was too sick to travel, Eti.

ETI: I don't believe that.

DELAL: Your brothers know its true. Ask your uncle.

ETI: I will. I'm sorry for saying ugly things.

DELAL: You were my favorite son. When you hurt me, you hurt yourself.

(ETI *nods humbly.*)

ETI: I sign this contract and our lives will change.

DELAL: We will see. You work with diamonds now. That has some future, even if you have to wear thick glasses.

ETI: You are a diamond, Ima. *(Pause)* I have to marry Sheva.

DELAL: She is less Jewish than this family. Don't lie.

ETI: So?

DELAL: Does she have Israeli papers?

ETI: Her grandparents were Jewish. Sometimes she wears a Jewish star.

DELAL: Kosher food? Do they work on Saturday? Is there a cross in her home?

ETI: No. *(She throws him a look.)* Maybe one or two.

DELAL: You're an observing Jew.

ETI: They know.

DELAL: Your father would stop dead in his tracks.

ETI: We will never know. That makes me very sad.

(A knock at the door)

DELAL: Sit down, Eti. Put on a strong face. *(She opens door)* Ezra.

(EZRA kisses DELAL twice on the cheek. FISHMAN is with him.)

EZRA: Shalom, Delal. I think you met Mr. Fishman.

FISHMAN: Hello, Delal.

DELAL: Hello. *(Pause)* Come in.

(They enter.)

EZRA: Shalom, Eti.

ETI: Shalom, Uncle.

EZRA: You're very hard to find, nephew.

ETI: I like it that way.

EZRA: I brought you a gift. *(Takes out a bag and hands it to ETI.)* A book on Olympic runners. I think I missed your birthday.

ETI: Thank you.

DELAL: Coffee?

EZRA: Please.

FISHMAN: Thank you.

(DELAL *leaves the room.*)

EZRA: Mister Fishman has heard a lot about you, Eti. He talked to your coaches and saw the videos of your events.

FISHMAN: Very impressive, young man.

EZRA: I wish Eti's father were here to see this. Mister Fishman wants to offer you a generous soccer contract. I brought your name to Mister Fishman. A very big opportunity for our family. You can travel around the world and make a prosperous income. The sort of thing that young men dream about. Be a very prominent Ethiopian in Israel and America. This is important, Eti, to black Jews worldwide.

FISHMAN: Well, to the matter at hand. Would you like to play for the United States?

ETI: Yes.

FISHMAN: Soccer will soon be a very big thing in America. And you've the ability to become the next Brazilian Pele with a million beautiful girlfriends.

ETI: Believe me, one is enough.

EZRA: (*To* ETI) Send the girls to me, nephew.

FISHMAN: (*Cheerful*) Your uncle told me about your eyesight.

ETI: It's just one eye as the day goes into night.

FISHMAN: Surgeons can do miracles. We can pay for the operation and you'll be healthy. A group of American doctors visit with you soon.

EZRA: (*To* ETI) The army doctors don't know what the hell they were talking about.

FISHMAN: Why don't we go out to dinner and talk about what this all could mean for your family?

DELAL: We don't like to go out to dinner.

FISHMAN: Well, we could talk here then. I've a photo album you might like to see.

DELAL: We are superstitious, Mr. Fishman.

FISHMAN: Really?

ETI: A modern world does not matter.

EZRA: *(Disapprovingly)* Delal...

ETI: I don't trust any doctors.

EZRA: These won't be like the army doctors. I thought this is what you always wanted?

ETI: I don't know.

DELAL: Leaving his family.

FISHMAN: You'll have enough money to come back all the time.

EZRA: Are you afraid of success? *(To DELAL)* He is free to choose his life at his age.

ETI: Maybe I am afraid.

FISHMAN: That's foolish, Eti.

EZRA: You had courage to come to Jerusalem. This contract is a blessing to your family and to Israel.

ETI: I had more courage when I was a boy.

(SHEVA enters without knocking)

SHEVA: I came to get you. Oh...you're doing business.

ETI: We're done.

FISHMAN: I'll leave the contract with you, Eti. Take your time and think about the beautiful things. We're talking two hundred thousand shekel signing bonus.

SHEVA: *(Half-discreet)* Two hundred thousand shekels...

FISHMAN: *(Winks)* Beautiful, beautiful dreams, Eti.

EZRA: You look sad, nephew.

ETI: I hope not.

SHEVA: We're going to marry.

FISHMAN: Mazel tov.

SHEVA: Now Eti can buy a pretty ring.

EZRA: *(To* SHEVA*)* I've seen you before.

SHEVA: Sheva.

EZRA: Hello, Sheva.

ETI: She's a singer in a club.

EZRA: I've seen you sing before.

FISHMAN: When is the wedding?

SHEVA: Tell them Eti.

ETI: I don't know.

*(*DELAL *enters with coffee.)*

DELAL: She knows what she wants.

SHEVA: *(Ever so sweetly)* I come from a good family. I'm carrying his child.

FISHMAN: Perhaps it's time I go.

DELAL: His father wants no part of this.

ETI: *(Clear rebuke)* Did father just talk to you, Ima?

DELAL: Without my husband, I fail.

SHEVA: I will convert, but my blood is already Jewish. A mikvah bath too. I will light candles each Friday night before I sing with my band. All grandparents Jewish.

EZRA: *(To* DELAL*)* I know a very nice rabbi who will work with her. You don't have to worry.

DELAL: *(Gesturing)* She's good. She's bad. Can't see it. It's in the air. Feel it with your fingers.

ETI: *(Mocking with affection)* Yes, I feel it. Incredible.

EZRA: *(Taking album and contracts from FISHMAN)* Here, nephew. I'll read this with you. Important decisions for you and your mother. And, if you're about to become a father, even more important.

SHEVA: Thank your uncle, Eti. Our world is about to change.

(ETI takes the album and contracts from EZRA.)

(End of scene)

Scene Twelve

(A club near Ethiopia Street, SHEVA ends her song after a few bars. Easy applause, spot light fades out. ETI, sitting near the stage, lights a cigarette. Mid-February)

SHEVA: You don't smoke.

ETI: You never see me smoke.

SHEVA: You're upset.

ETI: Yes. This was once the only Ethiopian neighborhood in Jerusalem a hundred years ago. Big Ethiopian Church in the center of Ethiopia Street. History laughs at us here. Now all the blacks are scattered in cheap boxes and tents on the city edge. Refugees in the Promised Land. We have a famous street, yet we are phantoms.

SHEVA: You always feel bad, Eti.

ETI: Things are moving too fast. *(Uncomfortable in the club. Rises impulsively)* I got to go.

SHEVA: Where are you going?

ETI: Somewhere to think.

SHEVA: Don't go. There are Russian boys in the house tonight. Keep me company.

ETI: Where? *(Turning)*

SHEVA: In back, but don't be obvious. *(Reaches for his arm)*

ETI: I'll talk to them.

SHEVA: Just stay here. *(Pause)* I have bad dreams too, Eti. Don't believe you're the only one.

ETI: Why did you tell my mother?

SHEVA: *(Aware of making a public scene, lowers her voice)* When your mother gets to know me, there will be sweetness. That is how my family taught me to be. It is our child.

ETI: You could have told me first.

SHEVA: I'm sorry.

ETI: And I never said a thing about a wedding.

SHEVA: You did once in bed. Sign the sports contract. Eat in fancy restaurants. Buy a new car. *(Rises)* Do we have to talk about this here?

ETI: *(To the club's onlookers)* That's right. Sheva and I are getting married! I'm the lucky guy this week!

(ETI kisses SHEVA.)

You want to see other girls. No, you are more righteous than a Yiddish rabbi. *(Pause)* You hate me.

(ETI grabs SHEVA.)

SHEVA: Then say you love me in your heart.

ETI: You know how I feel. I have a demon.

SHEVA: And what does he want?

ETI: To pull out my eyes.

SHEVA: Why?

ETI: Because I don't read scriptures and left Ethiopia. Because I can't visit the graves of grandparents and I beat up a Russian boy on the High Holy Days. Because I quit school and I had sex with you.

SHEVA: You're crazy. Don't say stupid things. I'm happy to be your wife.

ETI: If you have this baby, a demon might enter you, Sheva. I know demons and Jewish law.

SHEVA: No you don't.

ETI: You might have a miscarriage.

SHEVA: I don't believe in a punishing God. You don't really want this baby.

ETI: I'm too young to be a father.

SHEVA: Old enough to go into the army.

ETI:Any idiot can go into the army. (Pause) I'll be a ghost like my father. If I give you money, would you wait a year? (Pause) I'm not clever, Sheva. These are the words of a stupid boy.

SHEVA: Eti, our bodies have touched. You love me?

ETI: I do.

SHEVA: This is not our country yet, but you pretend it is. This is a land of white Jews. This government asks for our blood, but in secret it throws it away. Our blood, Eti. They think we're polluted, less than animals. They see you and me—primitive, unclean—pity such bastards. (Pause) I don't care about money. You say you love me each day. I like hearing it. I'm a pretty woman, so honor me wherever we go. If you gave blood to Israel, if you can sell a part of yourself to Mister Fishman, you owe me too. (Pause) You owe me something pure. We were virgins. We are Sheba and Solomon. We are the same flesh. You can't hate me for carrying your seed. I was a very young girl before we went to bed, Eti. You took a little girl from her home. You took a delicate feeling. *(Pause)* Help your family to like me.

ETI: I will try.

SHEVA: And I'll remove my tattoo. *(Points to the small printed cross over her brow)* I don't like my doctor at the clinic.

ETI: I can ask my uncle to find us a better doctor.

SHEVA: I want a wedding before the summer.

ETI: Will you be Jewish for this wedding?

SHEVA: You never asked me that before.

ETI: I'm asking you now. *(Affable sarcasm)* We'll get more gifts.

SHEVA: It's enough that I come from a line of beautiful African Jews?

ETI: I know all the high laws.

SHEVA: No, you see me as *"dohone"* —a cheap pot made of mud and straw. A Jesus Ethiopian.

ETI: I never said that.

SHEVA: You think it.

ETI: *"Dohone"* is a dirty word.

SHEVA: *(Overlaps his line)* *"Dohone"*. Bad Jew who turns gentile out of fear. *(Sincere expression)* I love you, Eti. You need to trust me. I can change for you in time.

ETI: I have to talk with my uncle about my eyes.

SHEVA: Is he a good man?

ETI: I hope so.

(End of scene)

Scene Thirteen

(HESHI's *diamond shop.* SHEVA *enters once the security\
door is buzzed open. It's raining and her hair and clothes are
wet. After a few moments, she catches his deflected attention.
Mid-February)*

HESHI: Can I help you?

SHEVA: Please. It's raining buckets.

HESHI: I can see, yes. *(Pause)* Are you buying or selling?

SHEVA: You keep the front door locked all the time—so
close to Ethiopia Street?

HESHI: Yes.

SHEVA: I'm looking for Eti.

HESHI: He's not here.

SHEVA: He said he was going to work.

HESHI: Did you see him today? *(Pause)* If you will
excuse me...

SHEVA: Do you know where he went?

HESHI: No.

SHEVA: Don't be rude.

HESHI: I'm rude to everyone, young lady.

SHEVA: Eti works very hard for you. You think you're
God's chosen people.

HESHI: Please, today I have a killer headache.

SHEVA: Eti is more devout than you.

HESHI: God knows.

SHEVA: We're going to get married.

HESHI: I know.

SHEVA: Eti's a religious boy, but doesn't show it. He
prays. He knows Torah. He said Kaddish for his lost

father. God respects him. And Eti can make a million shekels for a soccer team. He is a very special Falasha boy.

HESHI: Yes, yes, yes. All yesterday's news to me.

SHEVA: I am saving money to remove the tattoo. *(She points to the cross on her forehead)* We had to wear this in my old country to keep the Christians happy.
I have other tattoos elsewhere. But I'm taking up your time. *(As she is about to leave)*

HESHI: He's in serious trouble. Your boyfriend.

SHEVA: Trouble?

HESHI: He stole from me. I don't know what to do.

SHEVA: What?

HESHI: I treat him like my son. He has been better than my own son. This is killing me.
The police will get him before the week's over.

SHEVA: Why would he do that?

HESHI: Maybe you asked Eti to go shopping? He took a few diamond rings from my safe.

SHEVA: That's crazy.

HESHI: Talk to him. He doesn't need to ruin his life. He should return all the rings immediately and I'll drop the charges.

(End of scene)

Scene Fourteen

(ETI shining his shoes at home, talks to EZRA. Mid-February)

EZRA: Are you sure it's you child?

ETI: Yes.

EZRA: Do you love her?

ETI: I do.

EZRA: Do you want the child?

ETI: I guess so.

EZRA: Do you want to hurt your mother?

ETI: No.

EZRA: You know how your mother feels?

(ETI *shakes his head yes*)

EZRA: She loves you dearly. *(Pause)* Eti, you've a
bright future. I speak for your father. My only brother.
Everything we do involves risk. Have courage to take
wise risks. It doesn't really matter if you play sports in
Israel or in America. Or if you have a child now or in
ten years. What matter is your idea of freedom.

ETI: I know my freedom.

EZRA: I don't think you do. *(Pause)* This girl Sheva
means well. She seems devoted to you. Your mother
feels differently about Sheva. Maybe Sheva's trapping
you? You're both very young. She may be confused
about her identity. Somewhere in her family tree was
a long line of Jewish people. Sheva needs to wake up
to her heritage. *(Pause)* Our family tree has Jewish
definition.

ETI: Tattoos can be removed, Uncle.

EZRA: You're like your father, Eti. You are gullible to
many things.

ETI: I'm not gullible.

EZRA: Sometimes we're all gullible.

ETI: I've signed Fishman's contract. I want to be a
soccer star.

EZRA: You will. *(Pause)* If you marry, Sheva will stand
by you. *(Pause)* The political news is very bad now.
We are headlines. Street riots and protests about our
discarded blood. I want you to accompany me.

ETI: Why?

EZRA: We need to establish calm. You're a rising star.

ETI: I can't.

EZRA: That's not an acceptable answer. Why do you
look so scared?

ETI: I don't know.

EZRA: Travel with me for ten days. You'll be connecting
to our community.

ETI: I fear something dropping from the sky. Old
superstition, Uncle.

EZRA: You can't be superstitious in Israel.

(ETI laughs.)

EZRA: I wish you could talk with your father now. He'd
tell you to honor your people.

ETI: All right. I'll travel with you on your rounds.

EZRA: Thank you.

ETI: The government thinks we're diseased and
backward.

EZRA: Some people in the government, yes.

ETI: The land is holy, but most of the men in charge are
not, Uncle.

EZRA: You're right.

ETI: You are part of the government.

EZRA: I am.

ETI: Don't you feel shame?

EZRA: I could get paid a little more for the work I do.

ETI: Don't joke.

EZRA: I believe Ethiopian Jews have a home here with equal rights.

ETI: And Sheva?

EZRA: You can help her.

ETI: Sheva and I'll will be refugees again.

EZRA: Fishman can arrange a resident visa for you both in America.

ETI: And if my eyes turn into stones? I need an operation quick.

EZRA: They're getting worse?

ETI: Yes.

EZRA: What did the last doctor say?

ETI: He said maybe I could get better with a laser operation. One eye can be saved. Very expensive.

EZRA: Can you play sports?

ETI: One eye works. What can I say? You should tell Fishman everything.

EZRA: He'll find out soon enough. There's a Yiddish word—*basheer*— "if it's meant to be."

(Pause)

We're pressing our last Ethiopian airlift. You represent our success with Operation Solomon four years ago.

(Pause)

Come on, my boy. It's time you began to act like a mensch, nephew.

(End of scene)

Scene Fifteen

(RONIT *is visiting* DELAL. *MId-February*)

RONIT: Sorry to bother you.

DELAL: You like to visit our house, Ronit.

RONIT: I've been trying to contact you day and night.

DELAL: I visit my sister in Haifa.

RONIT: Delal, I'm not comfortable saying this—the police were looking for your son this yesterday morning and I thought you should know right away.

DELAL: *(Subdued)* Is he all right?

RONIT: Yes.

DELAL: Another fight with his girl?

RONIT: No. *(Pause)* There was a jewel robbery in the shop where he works.

DELAL: Oh God...

RONIT: I don't wish to panic you.

DELAL: Was he shot?

RONIT: No one was shot.

DELAL: What is it?

RONIT: The shop owner told the police that your boy stole three diamond rings. You know I am his job reference. The police came to my office. I told them about Eti's sports contract. I had letters from Fishman. It makes no sense for him to steal. This has to be a mistake.

DELAL: Oh God.

RONIT: Where is he?

DELAL: I do not know. Did you call Ezra?

RONIT: Yes.

DELAL: Sheva. She is responsible.

(*End of scene*)

Scene Sixteen

(EZRA'*s office. Mid-February*)

EZRA: In front of King David Hotel today, a well dressed man with a tiny bouquet was waiting for a blind date. Finally a heavyset woman approached from behind and he jumped. I could sense his great disappointment.

SONYA: My husband knows about you, Ezra.

EZRA: Good or bad?

SONYA: He's spreading mad rumors in my district.

EZRA: And that is not kosher.

SONYA: He feels humiliated. You met him at a charity function a few years ago.

EZRA: Yes, he likes to shake hands with a hydraulic grip.

SONYA: He's whipping up a ton of animosity toward Ethiopians. And he's very good at it.

EZRA: I'll talk to him.

SONYA: That would be homicidal.

EZRA: My homicide or his?

SONYA: He's not prepared for a divorce. Adultery is one of the ten commandments.

EZRA: Number seven at last count.

SONYA: Ezra...

EZRA: Is he a physical threat to you or to me?

SONYA: He was a bruiser in the army.

EZRA: Marvelous. *(Awkward smile)* Your other news, Sonya? I thought we would see more of each other?

SONYA: I wanted to.

EZRA: But?

SONYA: This is much too fast.

EZRA: We're not getting any younger.

SONYA: I'm past forty. I've lost my capacity to dream.

(EZRA approaches SONYA and hugs her gently.)

SONYA: It's all too confusing, Ezra.

(EZRA nods.)

SONYA: I can provide housing for a thousand Ethiopian arrivals. No more than that.

EZRA: Thank you, Sonya.

SONYA: You helped the Russian assembly vote. I'm returning the favor. I'm angry inside for you. Twenty-five thousand healthy pints of Ethiopian blood flushed down the toilet. That's how white Jews accept blacks. You can still eat at the temple's family table and I'll whistle Hava Nagila!.

EZRA: What should I do, throw Molotov cocktails at the Jerusalem Hospital?

SONYA: I would.

EZRA: A cargo plane is about to lift off this week from Ethiopia. Several weeks early. That, my dear, gets all my focus.

(ETI enters very distressed.)

ETI: Uncle...

EZRA: What?

ETI: There's been a horrible accident. Sheva was attacked by some Russians. She's in critical condition.

(End of scene)

Scene Seventeen

(Outside hospital room. Mid-February)

DELAL: They don't look good. Her parents. No sleep in two days. The doctor scared them. Her family went to eat. *(Pause)* Why are you here?

ETI: She might come out of her coma.

DELAL: God willing.

ETI: I'll wait with you until her family comes back.

DELAL: The police might find you.

ETI: I don't care anymore.

DELAL: I care. Go.

ETI: I didn't steal any goddamn rings, Ima. I have money now. Fishman gave me money in advance.

DELAL: The police will handcuff you and hurt you. You get sick in jail.

ETI: You'll talk to Ezra. He has sense. And Fishman will get me a lawyer. He will, Ima. Before the police get me. A smart lawyer will do things right. Here's the check. *(Shows it to her)*

DELAL: Too many bad things, Eti. The girl is very sick. I feel it in my bones. The police will think you did this.

ETI: Me?

DELAL: You and Sheva had fights.

ETI: Russians in her housing project. They taunt her on her way to school and to the club.

DELAL: Who told you this?

ETI: Sonya Gelman at the absorption center. She'll tell the police the same thing.

DELAL: Maybe. Your baby's gone, my son. She had a miscarriage. *(Pause)* Demons come and demons go.

ETI: I know, Ima.

DELAL: Blind like your father. You can pray. *(Pause)* Why Eti? Why annoy Ashkanazie Jews and their diamonds?

ETI: Did I ever steal anything as a boy? I saved Lebowitz's life from a street robbery. Did the police tell you that? *(Pause)* It's time you take my side.

DELAL: I will pray.

ETI: Sheva will recover. I will run away no more.

(End of scene)

Scene Eighteen

(EZRA's office. SONYA is already seated and he is standing. His face is bruised. Late February)

SONYA: So where is your Mister Fishman?

EZRA: He's late.

SONYA: You honestly expect him to phone the Minister's office?

EZRA: I'm a gifted actor.

SONYA: What time did my husband come to your home?

EZRA: Midnight.

SONYA: And you let him in?

EZRA: Yes.

SONYA: So masochistic?

EZRA: I must be. We talked. I poured us vodka. He blamed me for breaking up your marriage. Suddenly he got violent.

SONYA: He could have killed you, Ezra.

EZRA: *(Understated)* I sensed that, yes.

SONYA: This is not the end of it.

EZRA: He's not a handsome man, dear Sonya.
Yesterday, I bought a German built gun.

SONYA: Magnificent.

EZRA: It was either that or hire a lifeguard.

SONYA: Bodyguard. You should have gone to the
police.

EZRA: The thought struck me, but I'm uncomfortable
with the story. How did you ever marry him?

SONYA: We met in our twenties. He was so different

EZRA: Like Jack the Ripper.

SONYA: So where is Fishman?

EZRA: Ronit was supposed to bring him here.

SONYA: You're banking everything on him?

EZRA: I have no choice. Everyone said Fishman was my
best bet. And I sold him my nephew for a handshake.

SONYA: There are no more miracles, Ezra. You can't
afford this fantasy. *(Silence)* I'm waiting for a "get"
(Jewish bill of divorce) from my husband. I can't initiate
the divorce without his signature.

EZRA: Why not have a friend cut his car's brake hose?

SONYA: Don't put ideas in my head.

EZRA: I know a few nice kids you can hire for the job.

FISHMAN: *(Enters with* RONIT*)* Forgive me, Ronit was
driving me to the airport when we got your phone call.

EZRA: We haven't a moment to spare. Thank God
you're here. Mister Fishman, my dear friend from the
Russian Absorption Center—Sonya Gelman

FISHMAN: *(Shakes her hand)* Nice to make your acquaintance.

EZRA: She was extremely helpful with our housing problem.

FISHMAN: What the hell happened to your face.

EZRA: I walked into a B-52 jet.

FISHMAN: I can stay for only a few minutes. I have to catch the next plane. How can I help?

EZRA: You know the problem.

FISHMAN: Your nephew is in jail and his prospects look very unpleasant for us all.

EZRA: That's not the problem.

FISHMAN: I'll dispatch a lawyer However, his medical health is more troubling—according to my team of doctors. One eye is lost and his good eye is a bad gamble.

EZRA: I told you about his health.

FISHMAN: I don't like those odds. We'll redraft the contract and allow the doctors to make the call.

EZRA: Mister Fishman...

FISHMAN: *(Feigning absentmindedness)* But of course there is the refugee flight from Addis Ababa.

EZRA: I have no word yet from Minister Sharansky about landing rights in Tel Aviv. You promised me that he would get behind this!

FISHMAN: No one controls Sharanksy except his wife.

EZRA: My friend, fourteen hundred frightened Falas Muras have been airborne for two and a half hours. There are no seats, no food or water, no crew. It must land here.

FISHMAN: God willing.

EZRA: The Minister has reversed himself yesterday and refuses to allow the plane to land. That is what he's saying publicly. And I take Sharansky at his word.

FISHMAN: Under pressure by his Russian political party. You and Sonya know that.

EZRA: O K, O K. Let's compromise. Sharansky can grant fourteen hundred tourist visas to reunite the refugees with Israeli relatives for a couple of weeks. Which buys us time.

FISHMAN: It'll be a nightmare trying to round them up for the return trip. I already played that card with Sharansky.

EZRA: Where are you sympathies?

FISHMAN: With everyone Jewish. Do you want me to blame you for your carelessness?

SONYA: (Senses EZRA's anger about to flare) Ezra...

FISHMAN: Well, perhaps the plane will be diverted to an American airbase in the Mediterranean?

EZRA: That won't help anyone. (Trying to compose himself) Call Sharansky.

FISHMAN: Sharansky doesn't respect me any more. We hardly see one another.

EZRA: You're his chief fund raiser outside Israel.

FISHMAN: He doesn't take orders from Americans. Don't you get it? (To SONYA) Tell him. Tell him the truth about Sharansky. (Pause) Ezra, he doesn't give a shit about these people.

EZRA: Pick up the phone right now.

FISHMAN: Sharansky's never in his office after two P M. (Indicating SONYA) Why not your lovely colleague make the call?

EZRA: You've given his party a small fortune.

SONYA: *(Sardonic)* Call Sharansky.

FISHMAN: With the plane in mid-flight, it's a long shot, Ezra. Redirect the plane to Turkey, and let the U S military handle it.

EZRA: I'm not calling the plane down, Mister Fishman. Phone Sharansky! He owes you a large favor.

FISHMAN: You're fantasizing. Does the American Secretary of State know?

EZRA: Yes..

FISHMAN: That makes all the difference. *(Smiling warmly)* Bottom line—the plane will be allowed to land in Tel Aviv.

SONYA: Israel has turned away planes before.

FISHMAN: And risk American sanctions and horrendous press?

EZRA: I want an insurance policy. Pick up the phone.

FISHMAN: You know I spent a lot of money and political capital on this airlift already.

EZRA: Pick up the phone. Damn it, pick up the fucking phone!

FISHMAN: *(Slowly, reaches for phone on desk and picks up receiver)* This will accomplish nothing. *(Begins to dial)* It's ringing. *(He hangs up.)* I can't. I'm very sorry for you, Ezra. *(Pause)* I'm more important than a wayward African plane claiming a trace of Jewish blood. *(Glances at SONYA, and then EZRA)* I have my own high ethics. Remember that. *(Rises to exit)*

(End of scene)

Scene Nineteen

(Outside foyer of jail. A GUARD *walks* ETI *over to* DELAL *and* EZRA. ETI *is in street clothes. The next day, late February)*

ETI: They're getting my things from a locker and I can leave.

*(*GUARD *exits.* DELAL *reaches for* ETI'*s arm.)*

ETI: I don't feel well, Ima. Leave me be. *(He rubs his eyes.)*

DELAL: You look thin.

ETI: I'm training for Yom Kippur.

DELAL: Come, we'll eat at home.

EZRA: There's good news, nephew. Sheva came out of her coma.

ETI: *(Disbelieving)* We are still broken.

EZRA: Did you hear me?

ETI: Sheva...

EZRA: Is out of her coma. Her condition is improving. She will come through, Eti.

DELAL: She is stronger. You will see.

EZRA: You have to be patient. We'll all go to the hospital, O K?

ETI: Her family thinks I'm a thief.

EZRA: No. They know what happened. I've talked to the jeweler Heshi. The police found the culprit—one of his suppliers from Tel Aviv.

ETI: An Ashkanazic? *(Pause)* He came to visit me in jail. The jeweler Heshi. He couldn't look me in the face. Said a few words. Was very sad. Wanted to adopt me. Said I should come back to his shop. Hhe started to cry like he was my father. A Jewish diamond. He is Israel to me, Uncle. *(Pause)* And Fishman?

EZRA: He's gone. I'm sorry.

ETI: *(To* DELAL*)* My brothers and sisters are not here.

DELAL: You'll see them at home.

ETI: They should see a jail, Ima.

DELAL: *(Exits briefly)* I'll get your things.

ETI: *(Pause)* What happened with your airlift?

EZRA: The Ethiopians are in quarantine at the airport hotel. We don't know yet if the government will reconsider.

ETI: Reconsider? You're a different generation, Uncle. You've adjusted to things here. You have mastered the language and the barriers. You're like the white Jews. You have enough years to pass.

EZRA: Things are more complicated than that.

*(*DELAL *returns with a sack of* ETI*'s things.)*

ETI: Are they?

(End of scene)

Scene Twenty

(Triple split stage: ETI *visiting* SHEVA *at the hospital,* EZRA *meeting* SONYA *at a hotel bar, and* HESHI *at* DELAL*'s home. Early March)*

EZRA: Refueled and sent back last night with all 1400 wearing new sandals, caps and T shirts. Enough to make one puke.

SONYA: I'm truly sorry, Ezra.

EZRA: The Jewish Agency got involved. We had media coverage. The best negotiators. The Ethiopian community here knows the extent of what happened. They know Sharansky folded. And so did the Prime Minister.

ETI: *(In another area)* Sheva, I could peel an orange for you.

SONYA: God knows. Give it a rest.

EZRA: I can't.

ETI: *(In another area)* It's hard for me to eat. I used to like food so much before jail.

SONYA: Sharansky said he will soon go to Ethiopia for a personal inspection. That might yield five thousand visas. You did everything you can do. Finish your drink

(Light on hospital corner with ETI *and* SHEVA *in a wheelchair)*

ETI: I spoke to your mother. She knows about our plans. I like your mother. She has a very sweet smile, like your smile. But you know you look like your father. When we have children, Sheva, I hope they look like you. *(Pause)* I saw photos of my grandparents. My uncle gave his album to me. They're taller than I thought. They were giants, like your grandparents. Beautiful giants, Sheva. From the tribe that wandered far south. Their faces have pain, but I see eternal beauty. My good eye works. I have a magnifying lens. *(Shows it from his pocket)*

DELAL: *(In another area)* He's not here.

HESHI: *(With* DELAL*)* I'll come back another time. It was very hard to see him in jail.

ETI: And for distance I can use this glass. *(The spyglass is already in his hand.)* And the world looks perfect. If I could paint, I could show this to you.

*(*SHEVA *stirs,* ETI *peels the orange.)*

SHEVA: *(Softly)* Show me.

(Light on DELAL's *home)*

HESHI: I blame myself.

DELAL: Yes.

HESHI: Doing business with my cousins for years. How was I to know they would take from me? I nearly died from the news.

SONYA: *(In another area)* You know I have two grown children.

EZRA: *(With* SONYA*)* You once told me a long time ago.

HESHI: I cannot apologize enough. I want Eti back in my shop. I want to cater the wedding, Mrs Shlomo. I have to make up the sin. Please understand. I know how to be a better man as God is my witness.

(Light on hotel bar)

SONYA: I let on about you. They were upset.

EZRA: Because of your husband?

SONYA: No, because you were born in Ethiopia.

ETI: *(In another area)* I still like diamonds, Sheva.

SHEVA: *(With* ETI*)* So do I.

ETI: If I go back to school, we'll have to get by with just a few shekels.

EZRA: I'm sorry if I caused you turmoil.

DELAL: *(In another area)* My son has a future.

SONYA: I want to keep seeing you, Ezra. I don't care about the risks.

(She kisses him)

(Light on DELAL's *home)*

HESHI: It is a bright future, my dear woman. *(Pause)* I'll come back tomorrow. Thank you kindly.

(Light on hospital)

SHEVA: You're the fastest runner in the world, my Eti.

ETI: I love you, Sheva. Thank you for finding me.
(Pause) I've been lost for a long time.

(Leans over wheelchair to kiss her)

END OF PLAY

GLOSSARY

FALASHA—Literal meaning, foreigner, the term referring to Jewish Ethiopians.

BETA ISRAELI—The term that Jewish Ethiopians call themselves.

FALAS MURA—Historical Jewish Ethiopians who have converted to Christianity.

ASHKANAZIE—The family of Jews from Central Europe and Russia.

KNESSET—The Israeli elected parliament.

MISHIGUNAH—Yiddish term for "crazy".

ARIEL SHARON—Cabinet Minister & Army Officer who led 1980s Lebanon invasion.

NATAN SHARANSKY—Cabinet Minister & celebrated Soviet emigre.

MIKVAH—purification bath for Jewish women.

OPERATION MOSES—First Israeli emergency airlift from Ethiopia/Sudan in 1984.

OPERATION SOLOMON—Israeli airlifts from Ethiopia in 1991.

STAR OF DAVID—6 Point Jewish Star, symbol of Jewish culture and statehood.

QUARA DISTRICT—Region in Ethiopia where remaining Jews reside.

DOHONE—Derogatory word for frightened African Jews who converted to Christianity.

LAW OF RETURN—Israel's policy to allow any Jew an unimpeded entry into Israel.

BRIEF SUMMARY OF THE FALASHA/ BETA ISRAEL

Beta Israel people claim lineage to Menilek 1, the known son of King Solomon and the Queen of Sheba. It is assumed, however, that their ancestors came from Ethiopia's Agew peoples who were converted by southern Arabian Jews around the turn of the Christian Era. These Ethiopian Jews observed Jewish practices after the conversion of the Ethiopian Kingdom of Aksum to Christianity in the 4th Century, and sadly they were persecuted and driven back to northern Ethiopia. There were sustained attempts to destroy Beta Israel in the 15th and 16th centuries, but they kept their autonomy until the 17th century when they lost their lands. In more modern times Beta Israel's situation improved in Ethiopia's Lake Tana area where the men work as farmers, weavers and blacksmiths and the women raise children and fashion pottery.

Beta Israel have a Bible (although without the accompanying Talmudic laws) and prayer book written in the ancient Ethiopian language Ge'ez. Sabbath is observed along with many dietary laws and circumcision rites are consistently practiced. Synagogue services are conducted by "kohanim" rabbis and many of the major Jewish holidays are celebrated.

The controversy of how many Ethiopian Jews have
immigrated in Israel during the 1980-1992 years
continues to this day. According to the Israel's Central
Bureau of Statistics, almost 45,000 Ethiopians reached
the nation during that period. This should be seen in
contrast to the 1952-1979 era with under 500 Ethiopian
arrivals. Unquestionable, most of these people were
Beta Israel/Falasha, while others were either lacking
significant Jewish affiliation or were explicit Christians.
The most dramatic Israeli evacuation, Operation
Moses (November 1984—January 1985) airlifted over
6500 lives routed through neighboring Sudan. Israel's
Operation Solomon (May 1991) brought over around
14,000 Jews from Ethiopia's capital Addis Ababa.

In an Israeli newspaper expose in the winter of 1996,
these Falasha immigrants were greatly humiliated
by the Israeli government's mass discarding of all
donated Ethiopian blood. Clearly, the government's
chief fear was HIV contamination which was and is
so prevalent in Africa. One immediate consequence
was a violent protest by 10,000 Falasha individuals
which led to injuries in more than 70 demonstrators
and police officers. These numbers accounted for 1/6th
of the 60,000 Falasha community in Israel at the time.
Subsequently, the government issued a commission
of inquiry chaired by former Israeli president Yitzhak
Navon.

In light of the Falasha phenomenon, the most pressing
ongoing issue in Israel concerns how many remaining
Jews are in Ethiopia's Quara district and also how to
view Ethiopia's Falas Mura community which has
strong anthropological claims to Beta Israel. Falas Mura
people were either forced into Christian conversions
or chose to convert over the last few generations.
Typically, many Falas Mura individuals wear Christian
cross tatoos on their faces as a public sign of fidelity.

Because of their discernible ties to Beta Israel/Falasha, many Falas Mura families claim today that they are hounded and despised by their Ethiopian neighbors

www.ingramcontent.com/pod-product-compliance
Lightning Source LLC
Chambersburg PA
CBHW052216090426
42741CB00010B/2565